DOGS BODIES

Ralph STEADman

PADDINGTON PRESS LTD NEW YORK & LONDON

LCCN 76-62523
ISBN 0 448 22975 7
Copyright © 1977 Ralph Steadman
All rights reserved

Printed in England by Drydens Printers Ltd., London

IN THE UNITED STATES
PADDINGTON PRESS LTD.
Distributed by
GROSSET & DUNLAP

IN THE UNITED KINGDOM
PADDINGTON PRESS LTD.

IN CANADA
Distributed by
RANDOM HOUSE OF CANADA LTD.

IN AUSTRALIA
Distributed by
ANGUS & ROBERTSON PTY. LTD.

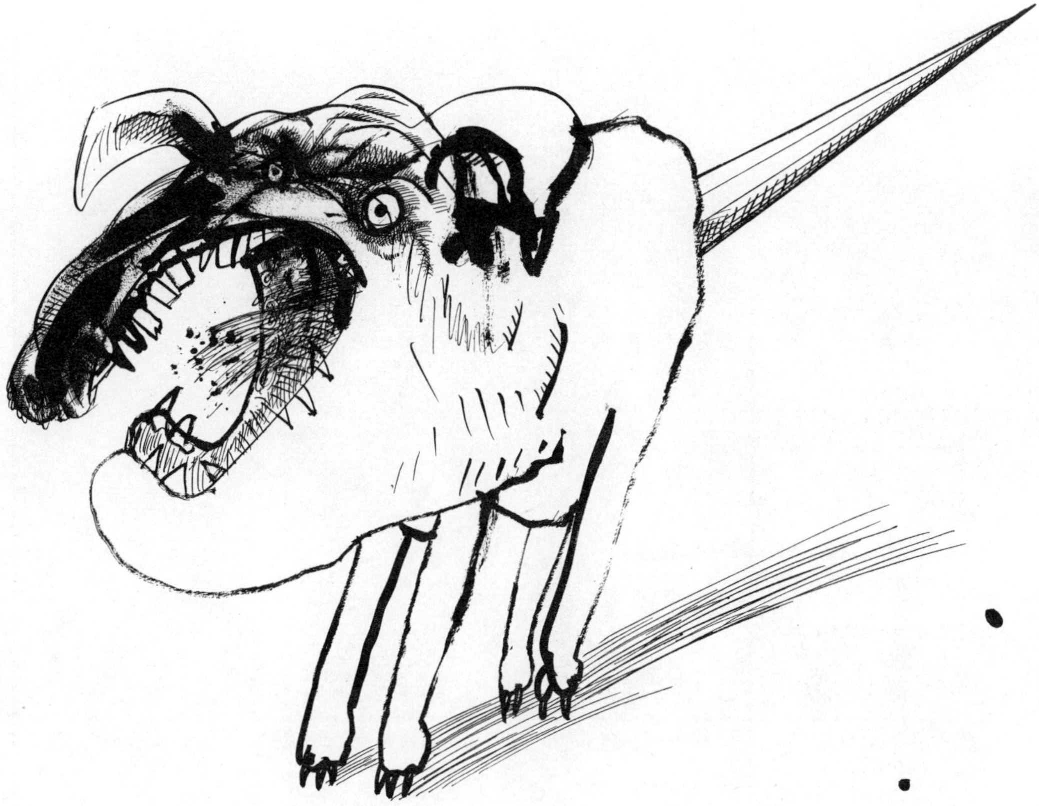

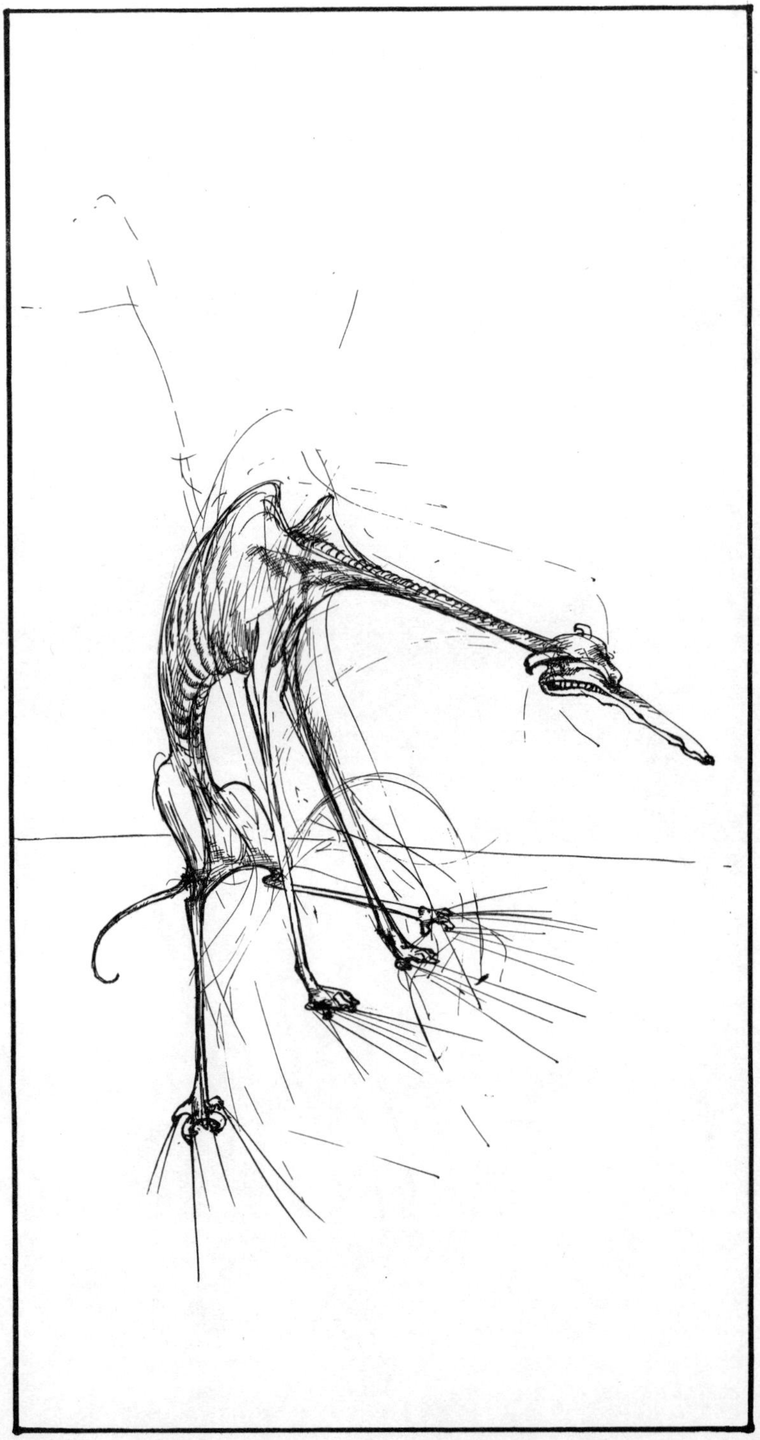

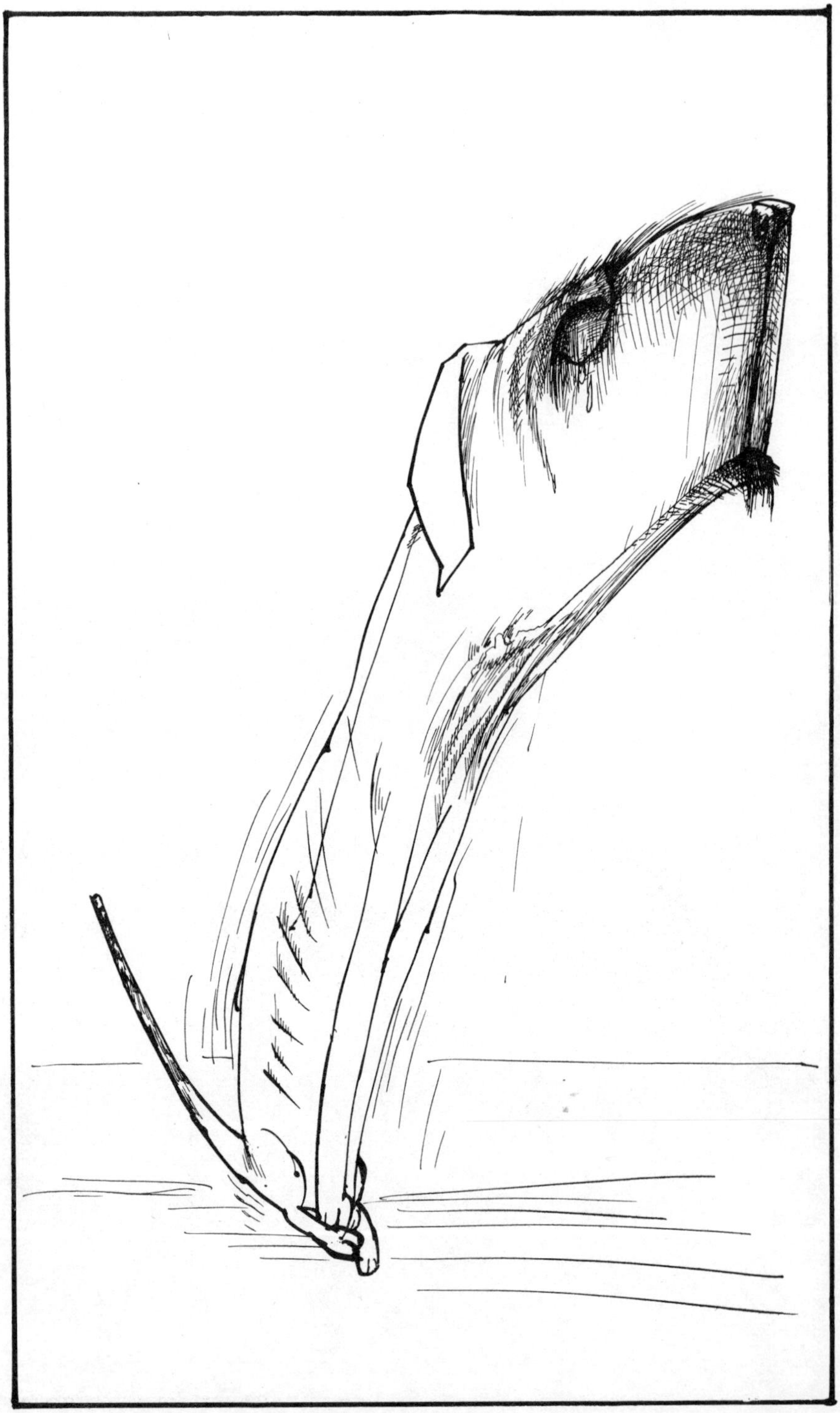

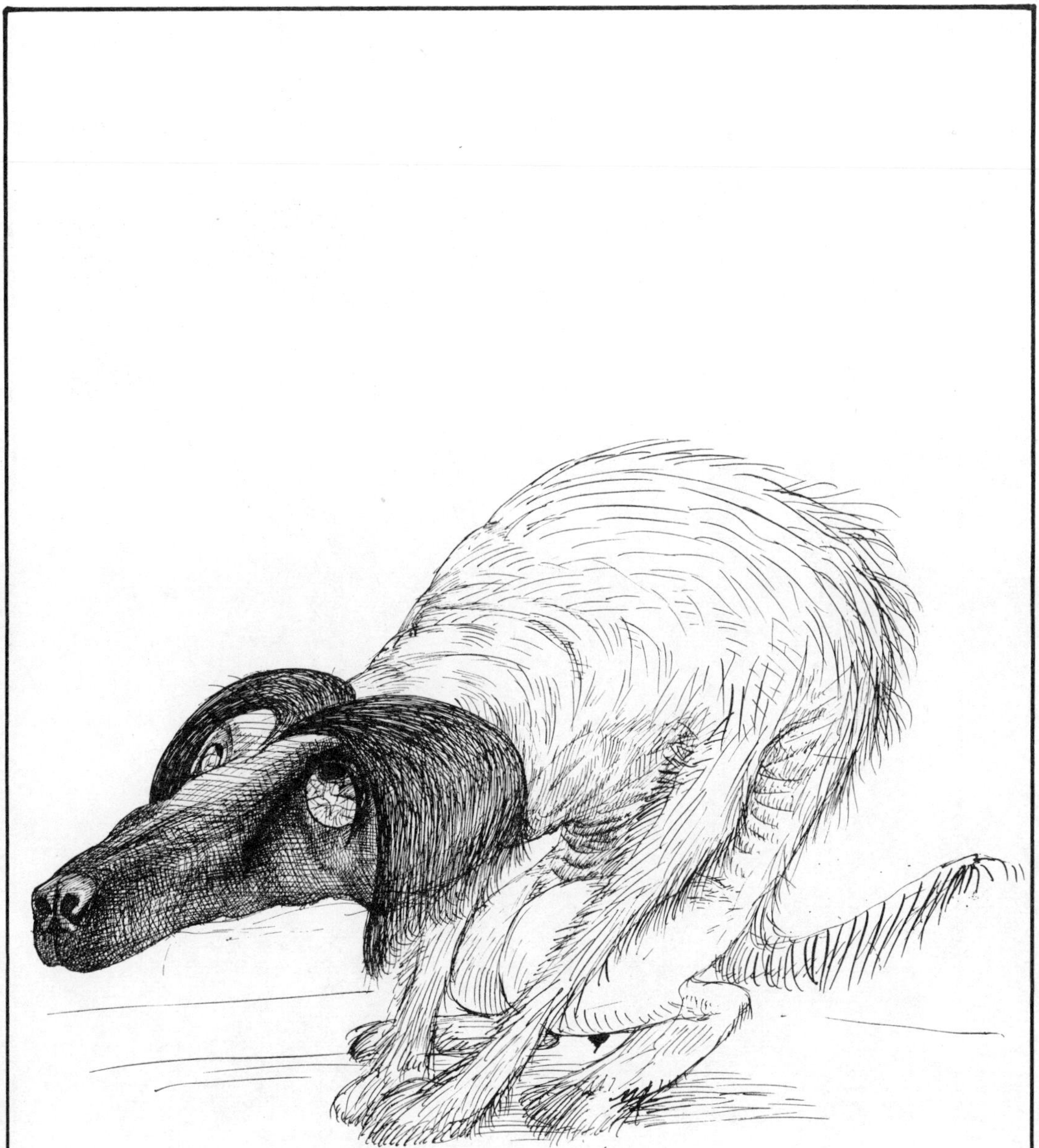

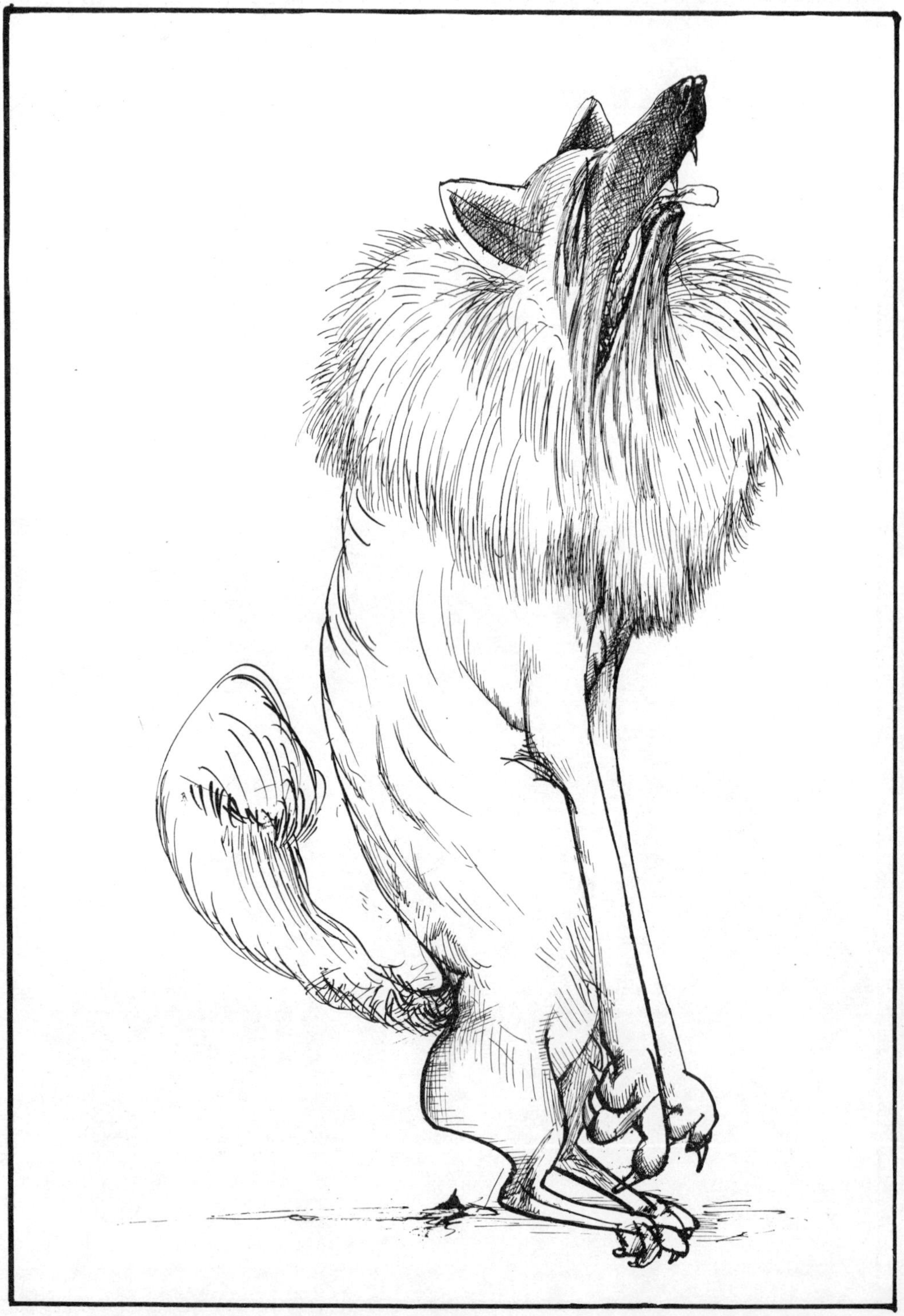

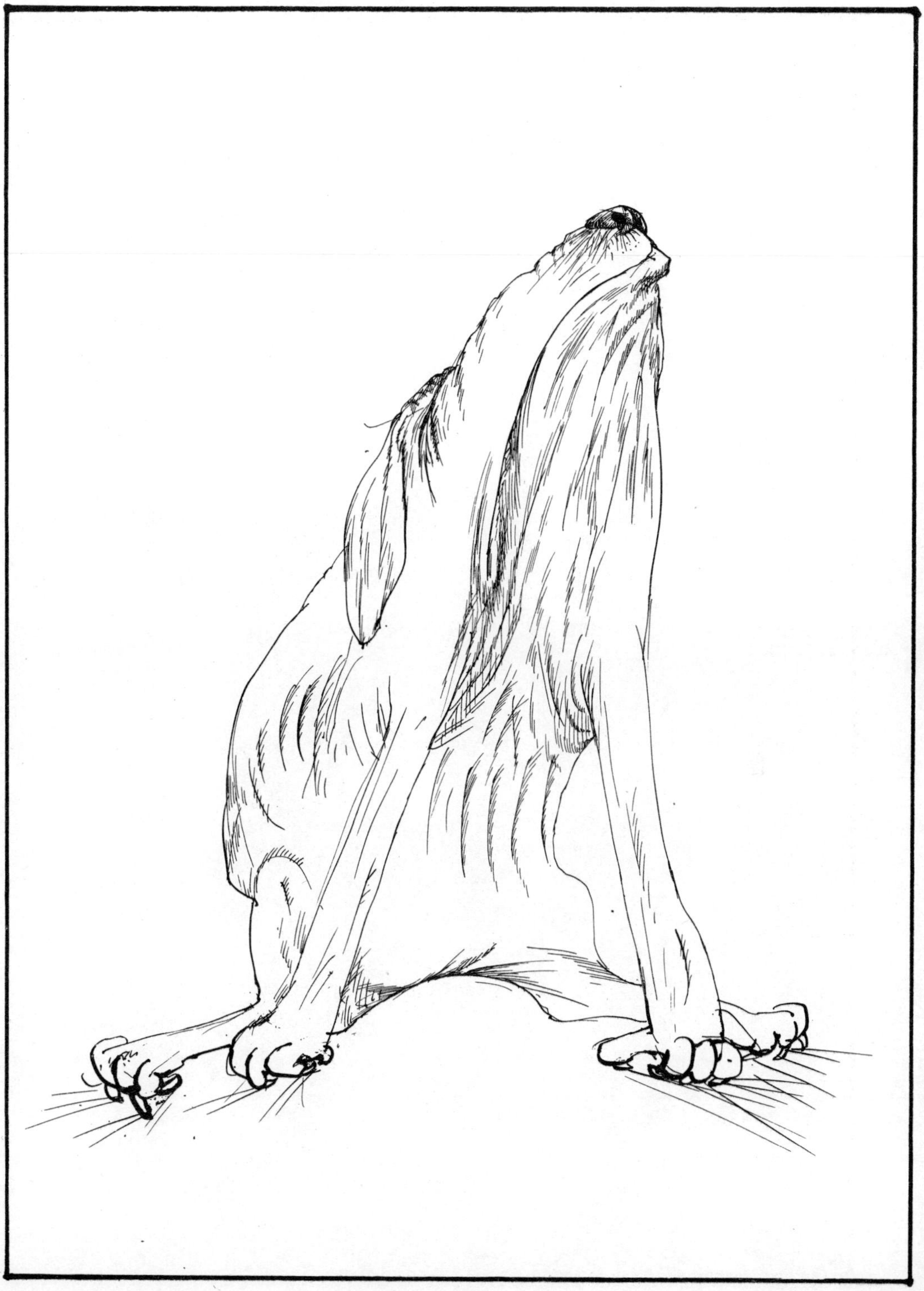

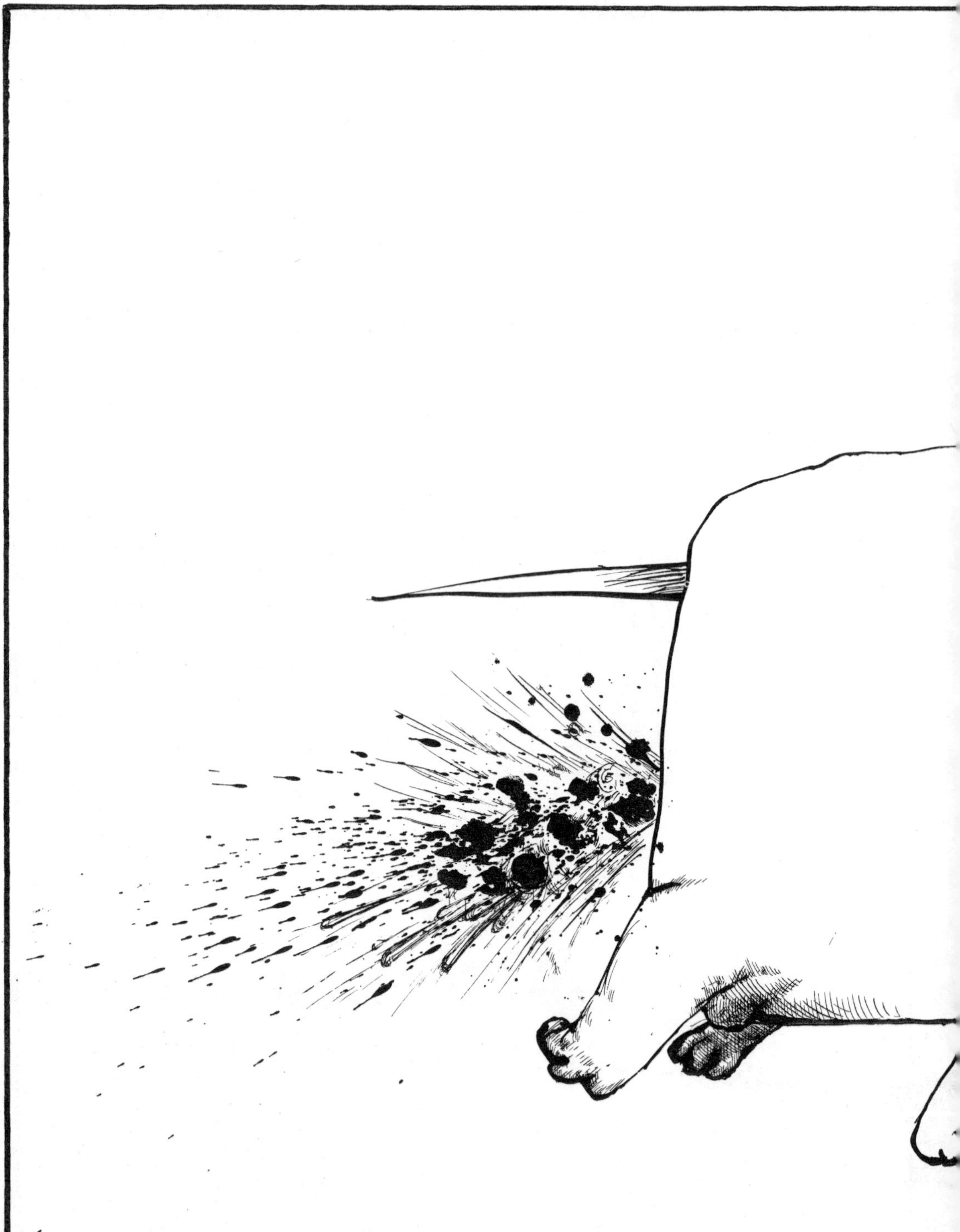

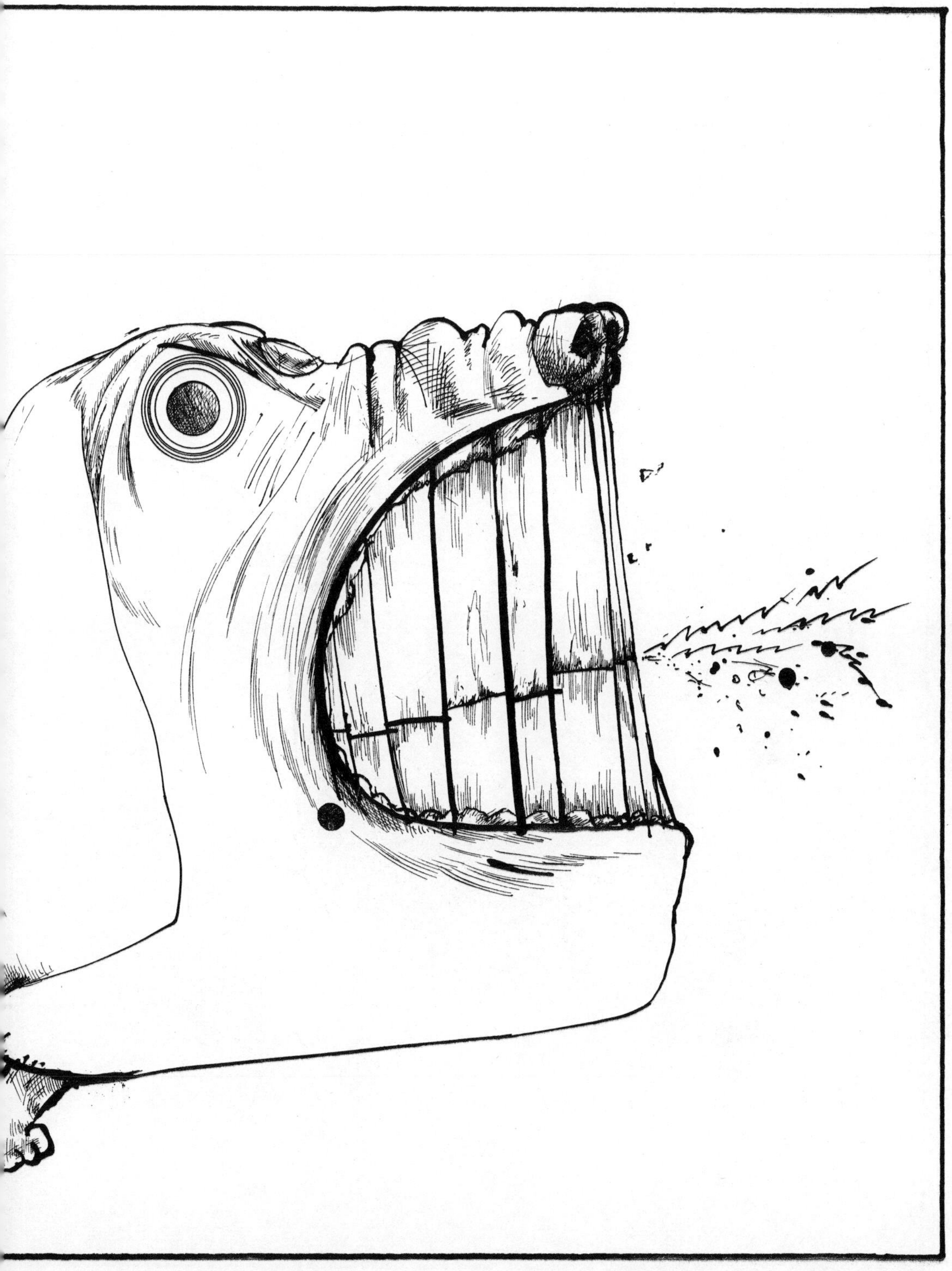

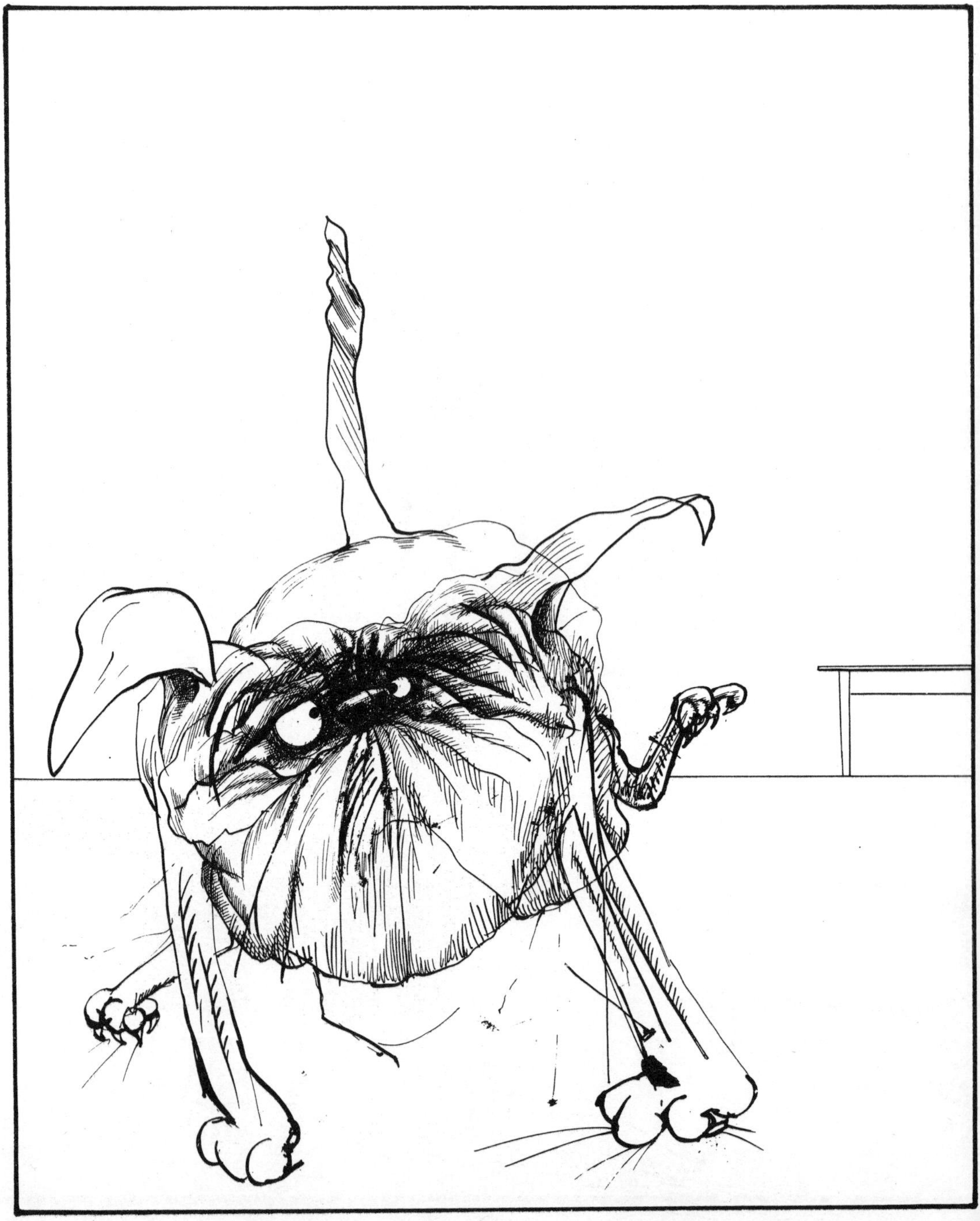

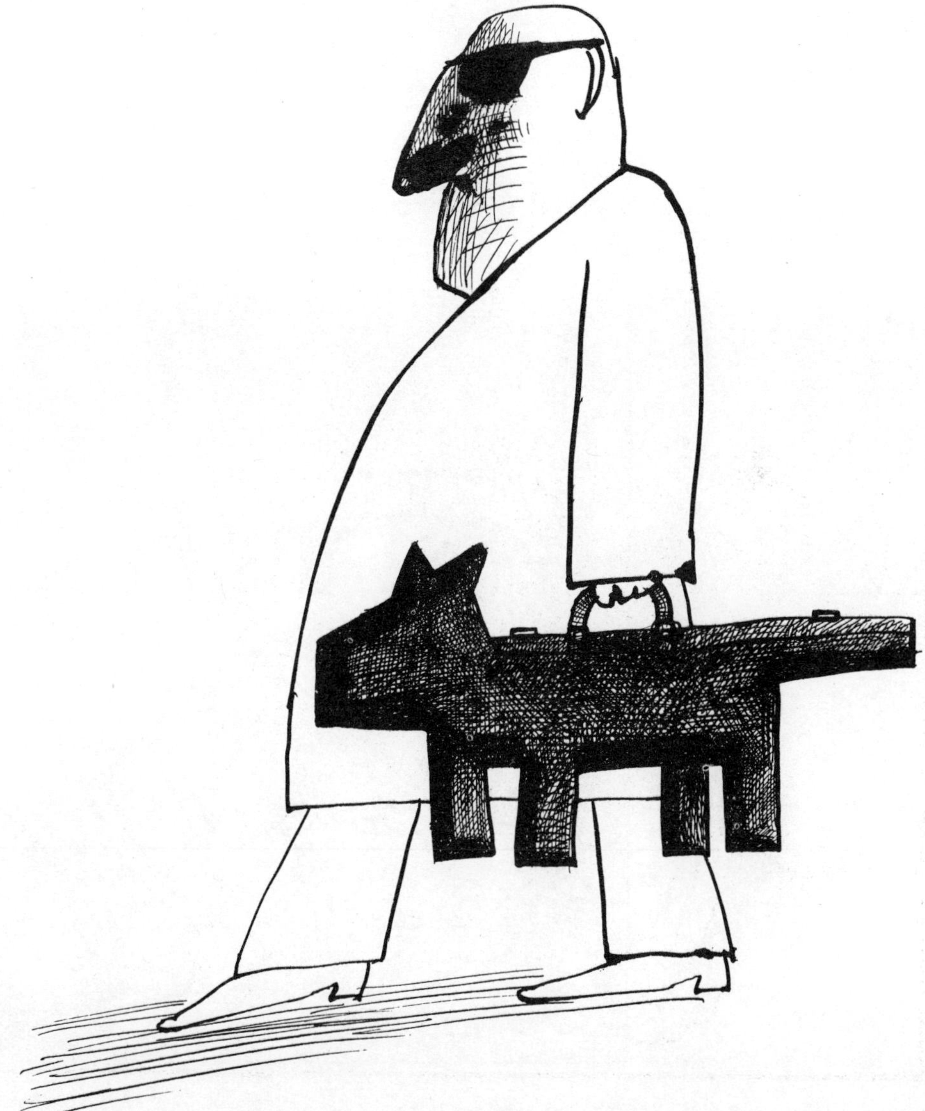

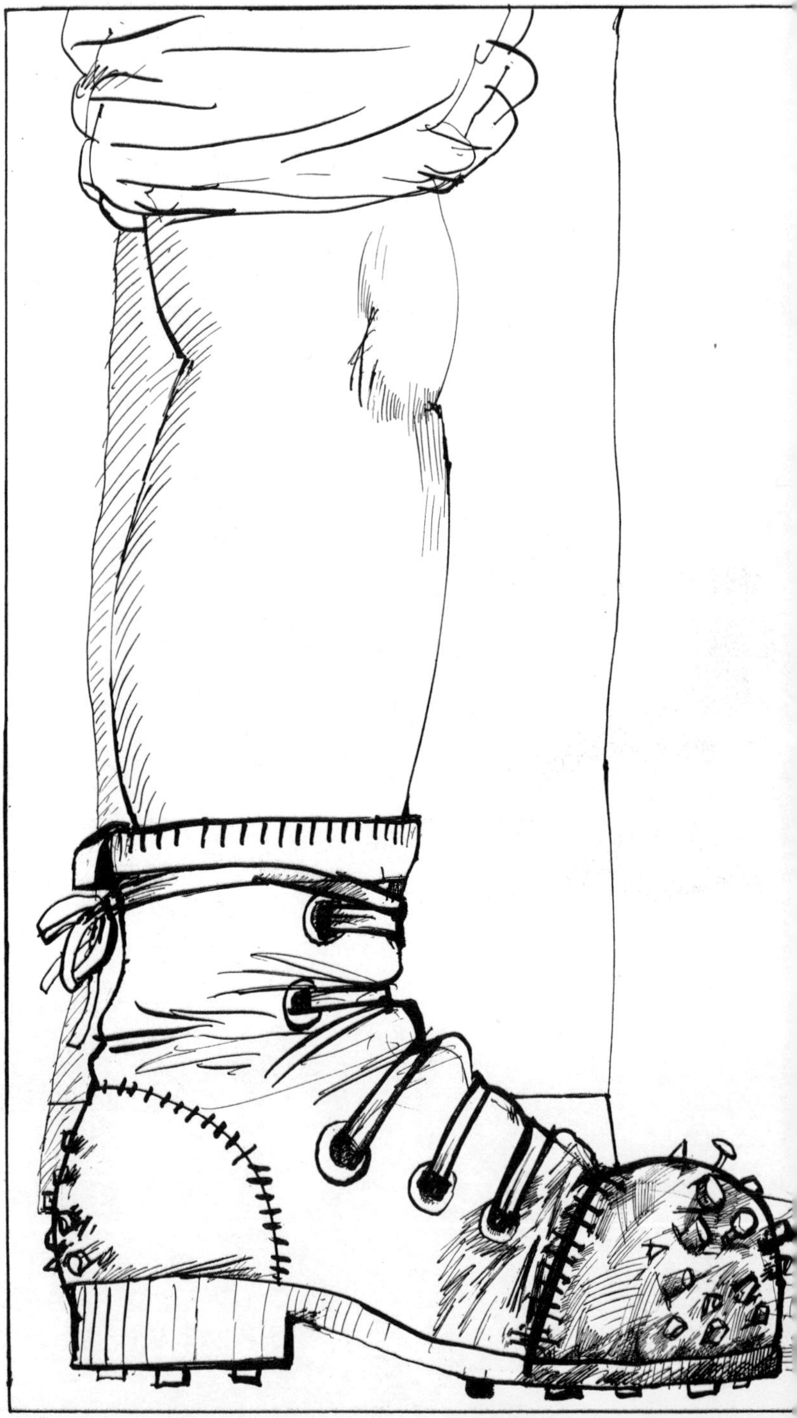

HOW TO TREAT YOUR DOG AND DISCIPLINE HIM. **1.**
DON'T BE FOOLED BY THE LOOK — HE'S HOPING YOU WILL SAY "THERE, THERE, DON'T DO IT AGAIN" SO THAT HE CAN DO IT AGAIN —— PUT THE *BOOT IN RIGHT AWAY; DON'T HESITATE FOR A MOMENT!

* CORRECTIVE BOOTS CAN BE OBTAINED FROM ALL GOOD PET SHOPS — RIGHT OR LEFT FEET.

HOW TO DISCIPLINE YOUR DOG. 2.

WAIT UNTIL YOUR DOG IS IN THE BEGGING POSITION THEN SMARTLY DROP A PICKLE DOWN HIS OPEN GULLET — HE'LL NEVER BEG AGAIN.

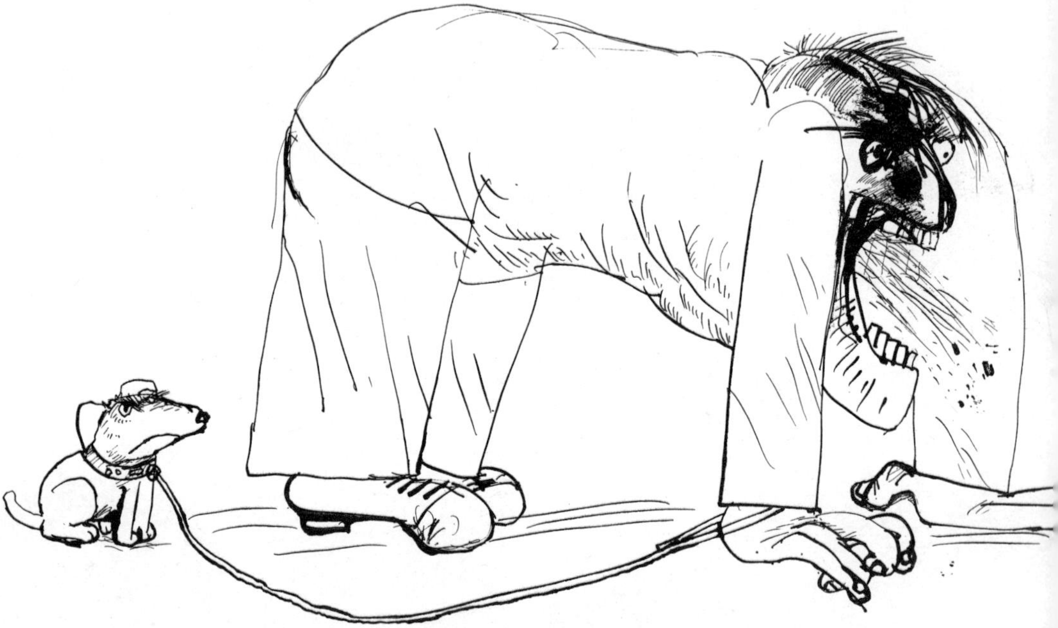

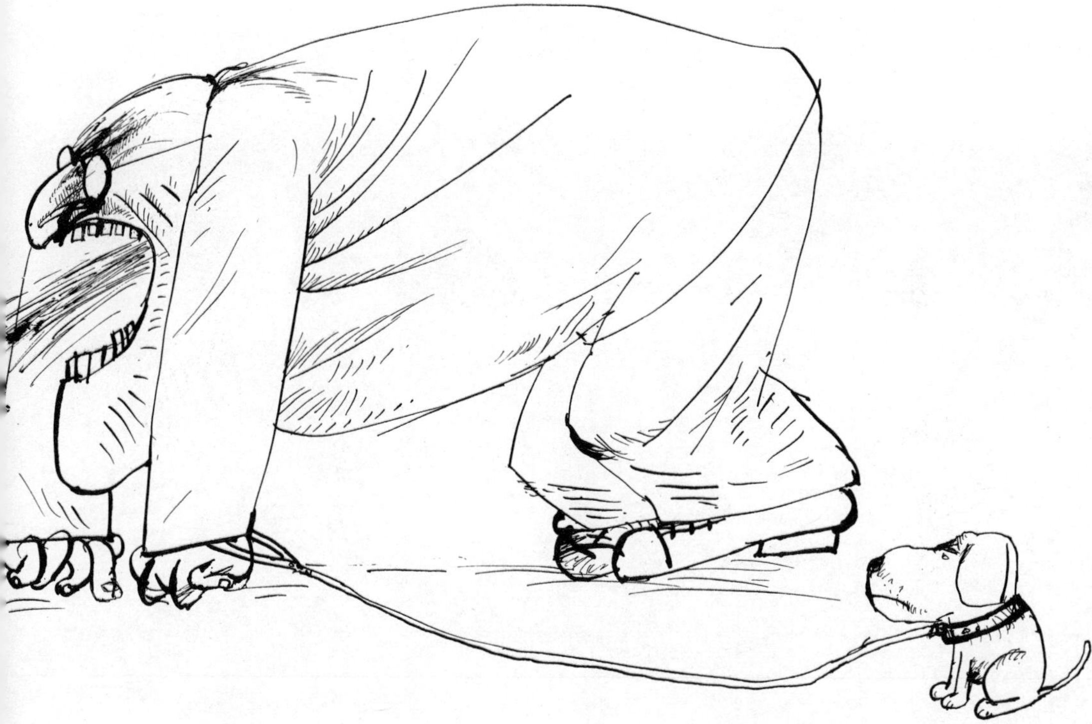

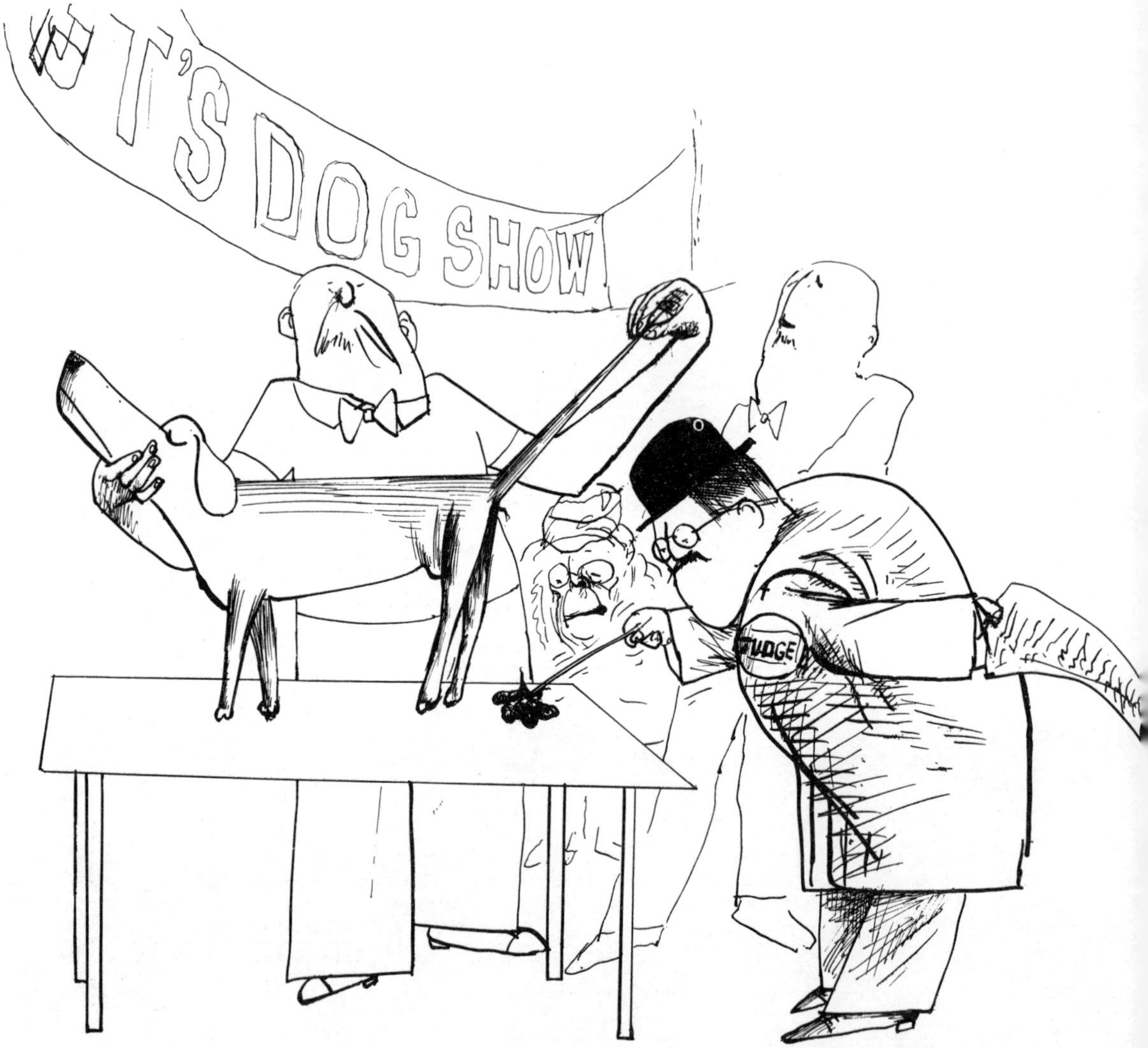
T'S DOG SHOW
JUDGE

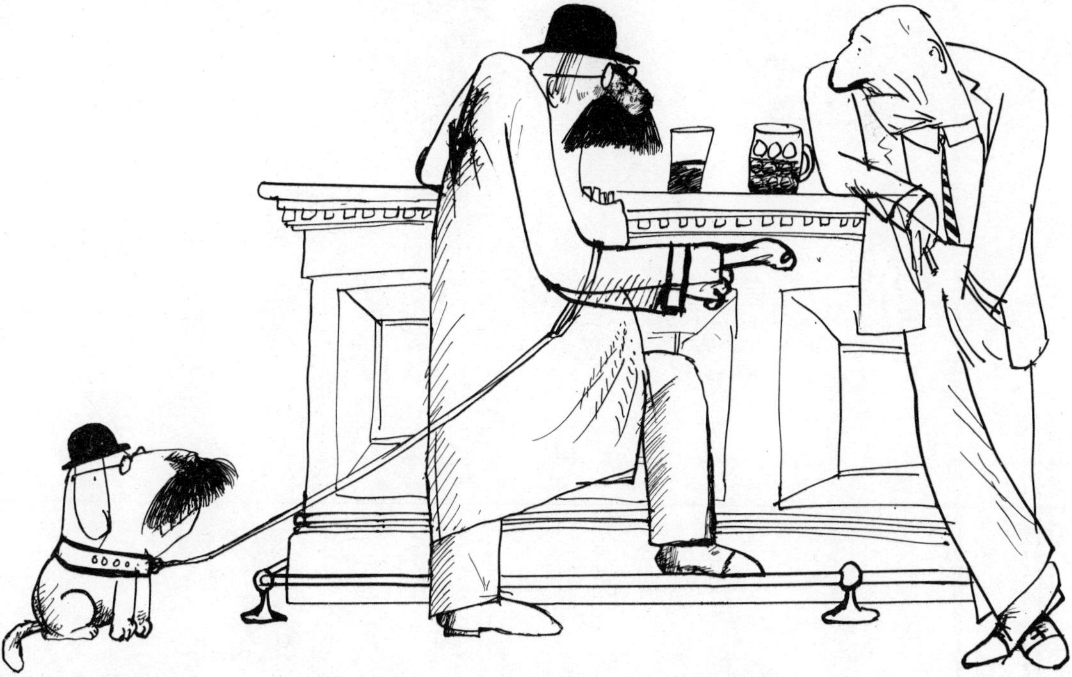

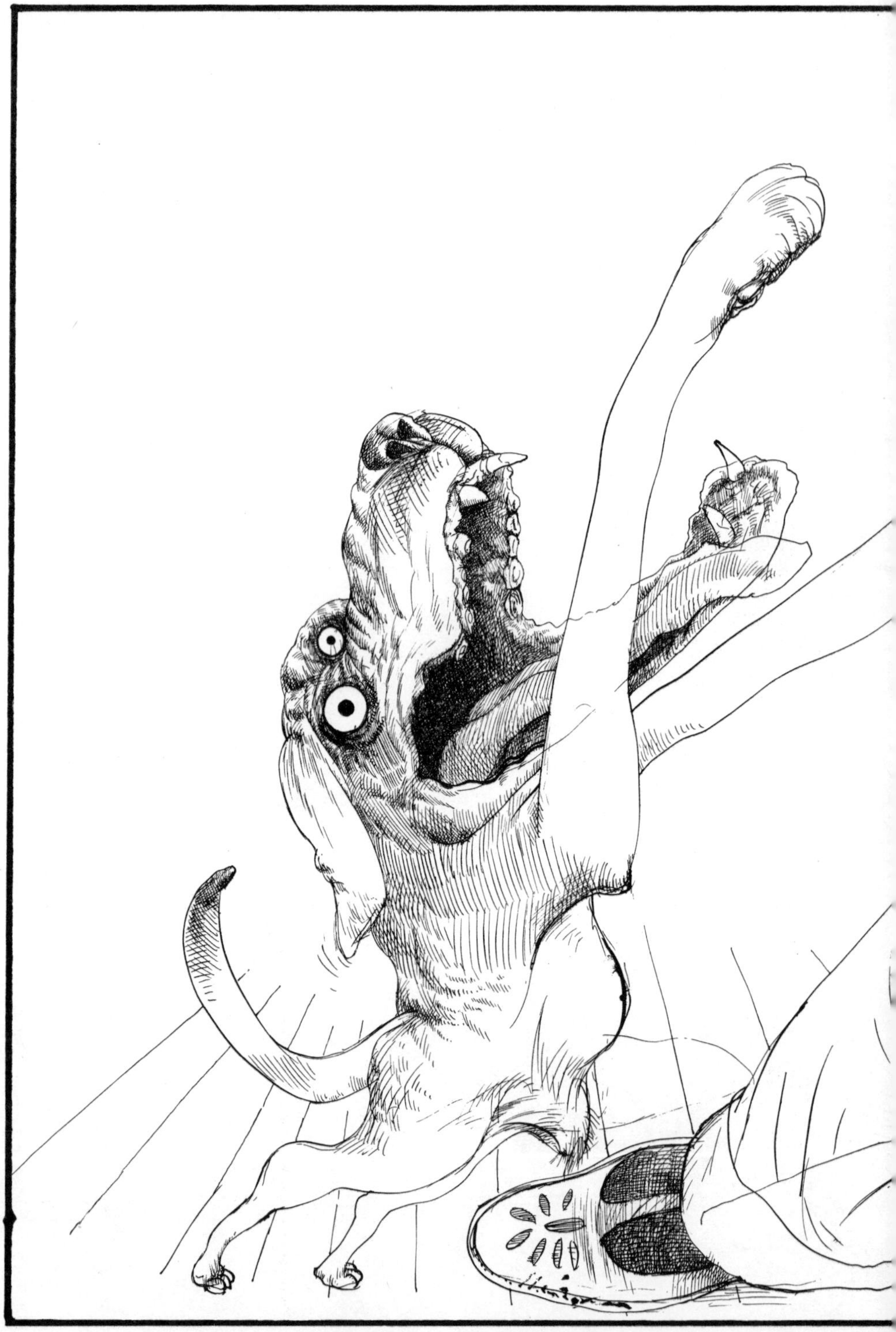

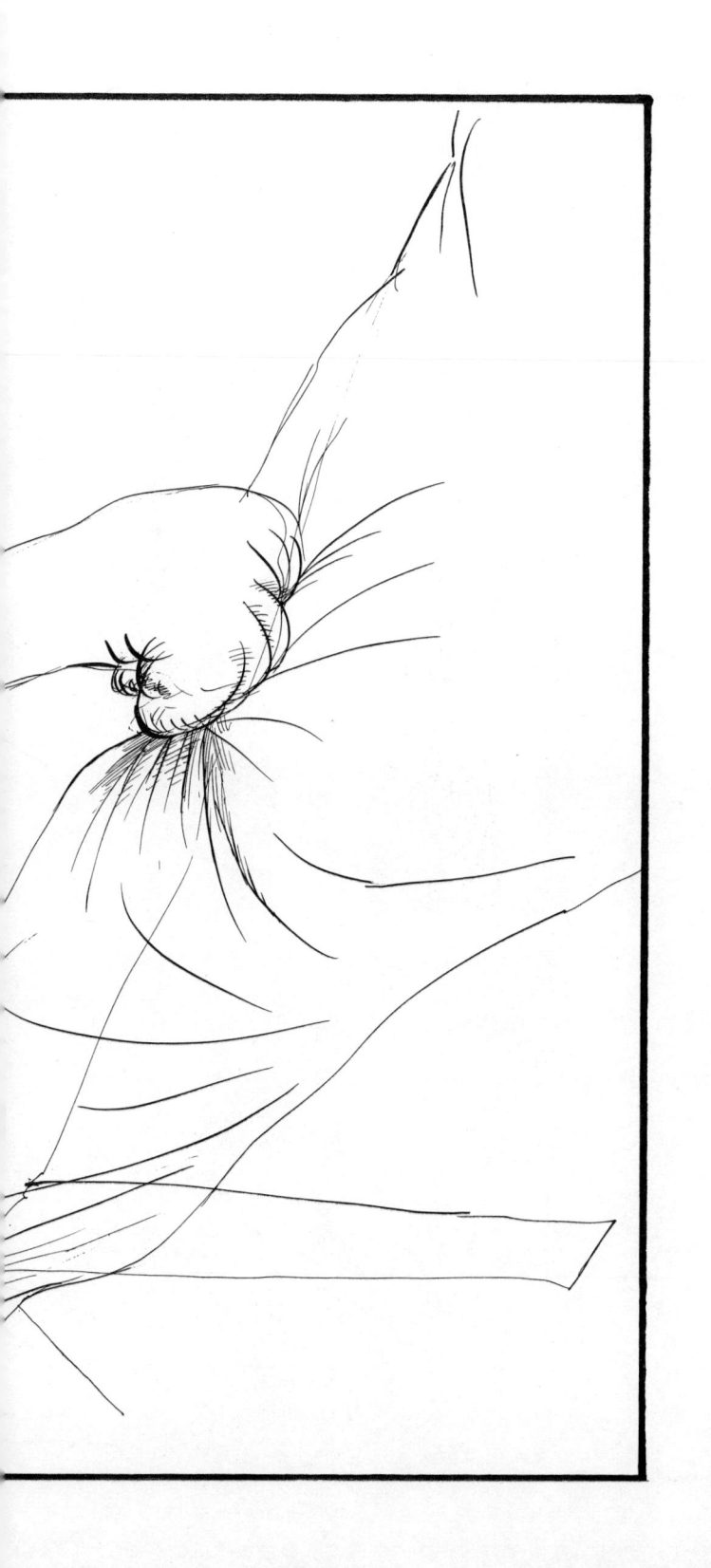

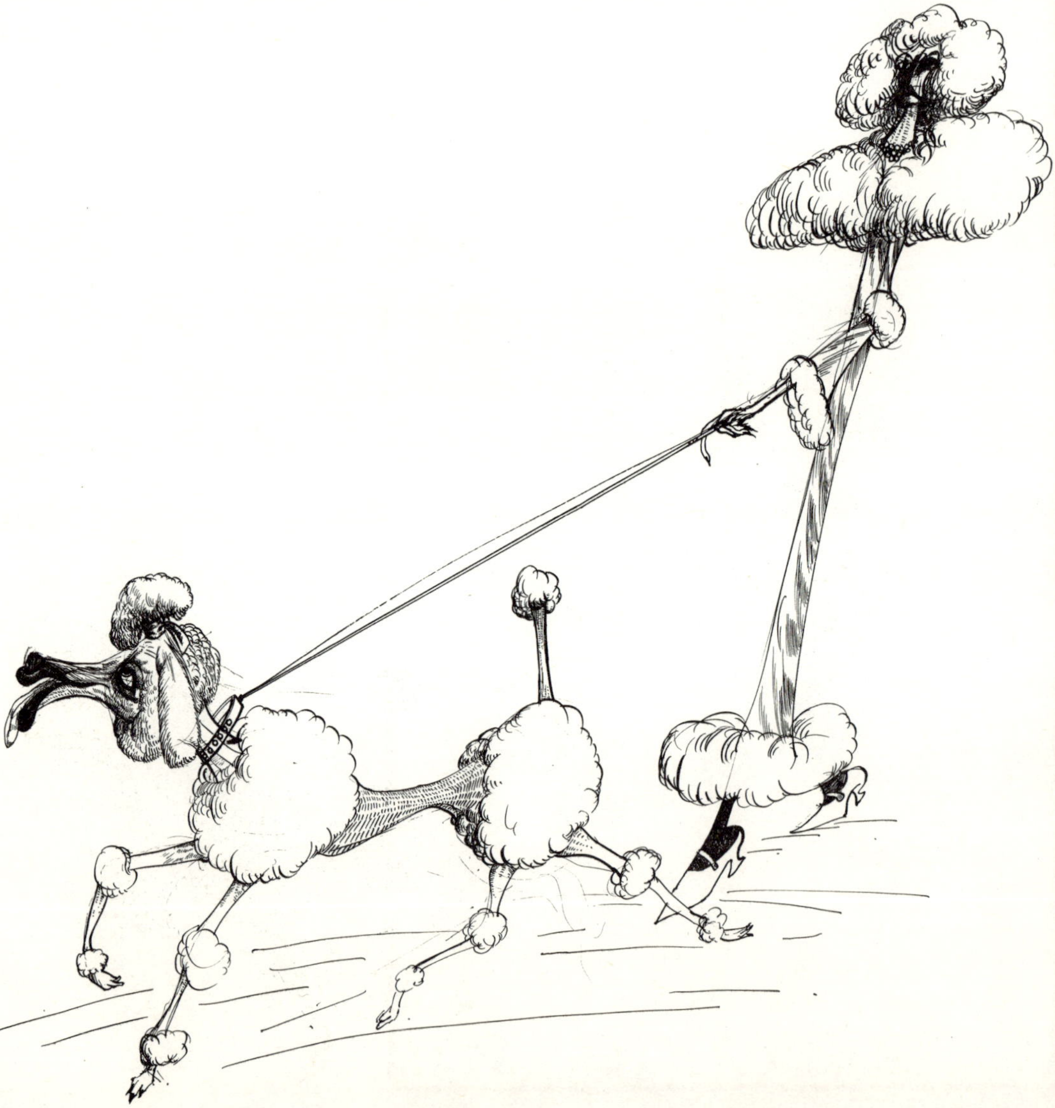

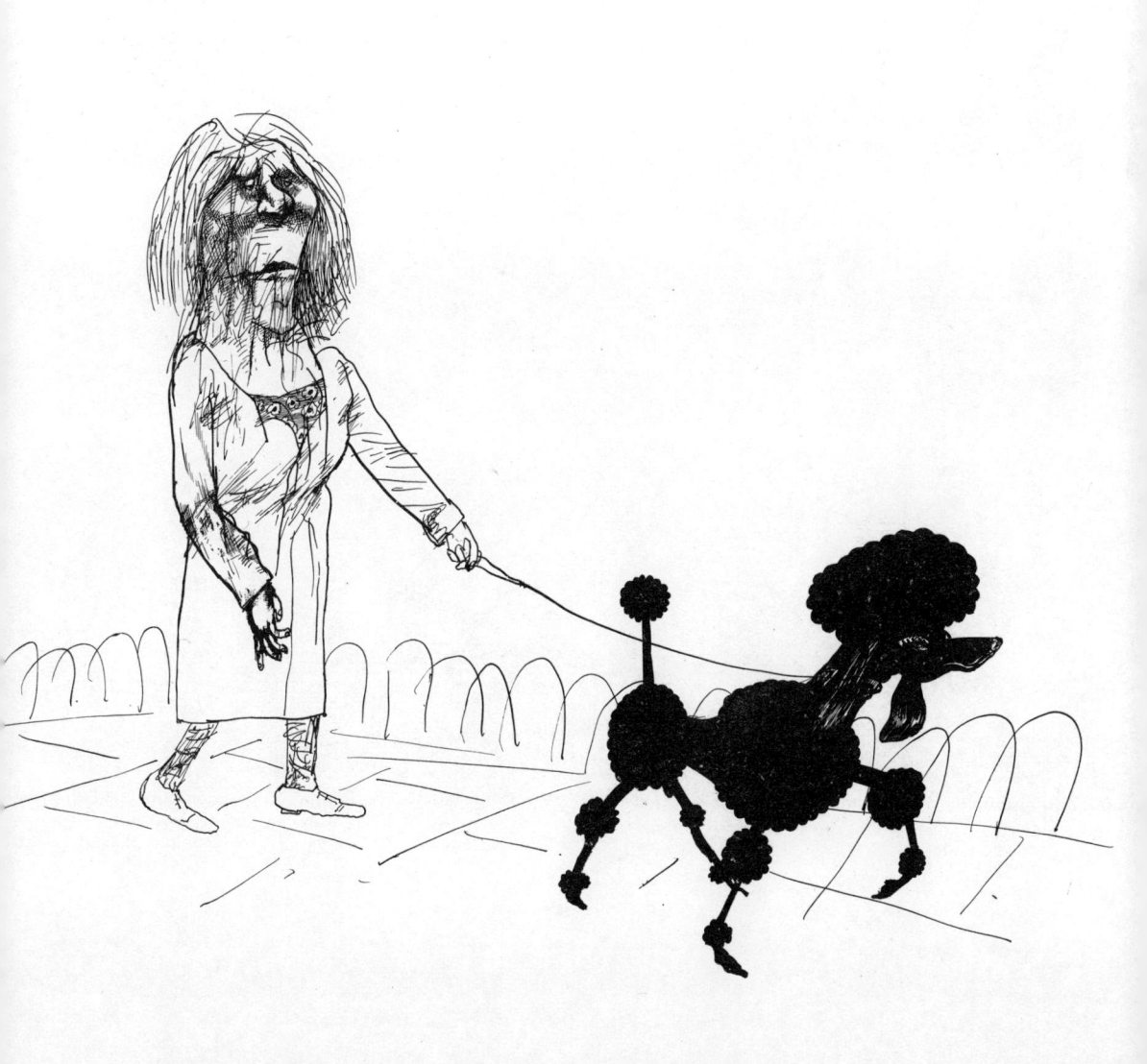

Man leading his blind dog, specially bought for him by ~~special~~ ~~the~~ kindly donations.

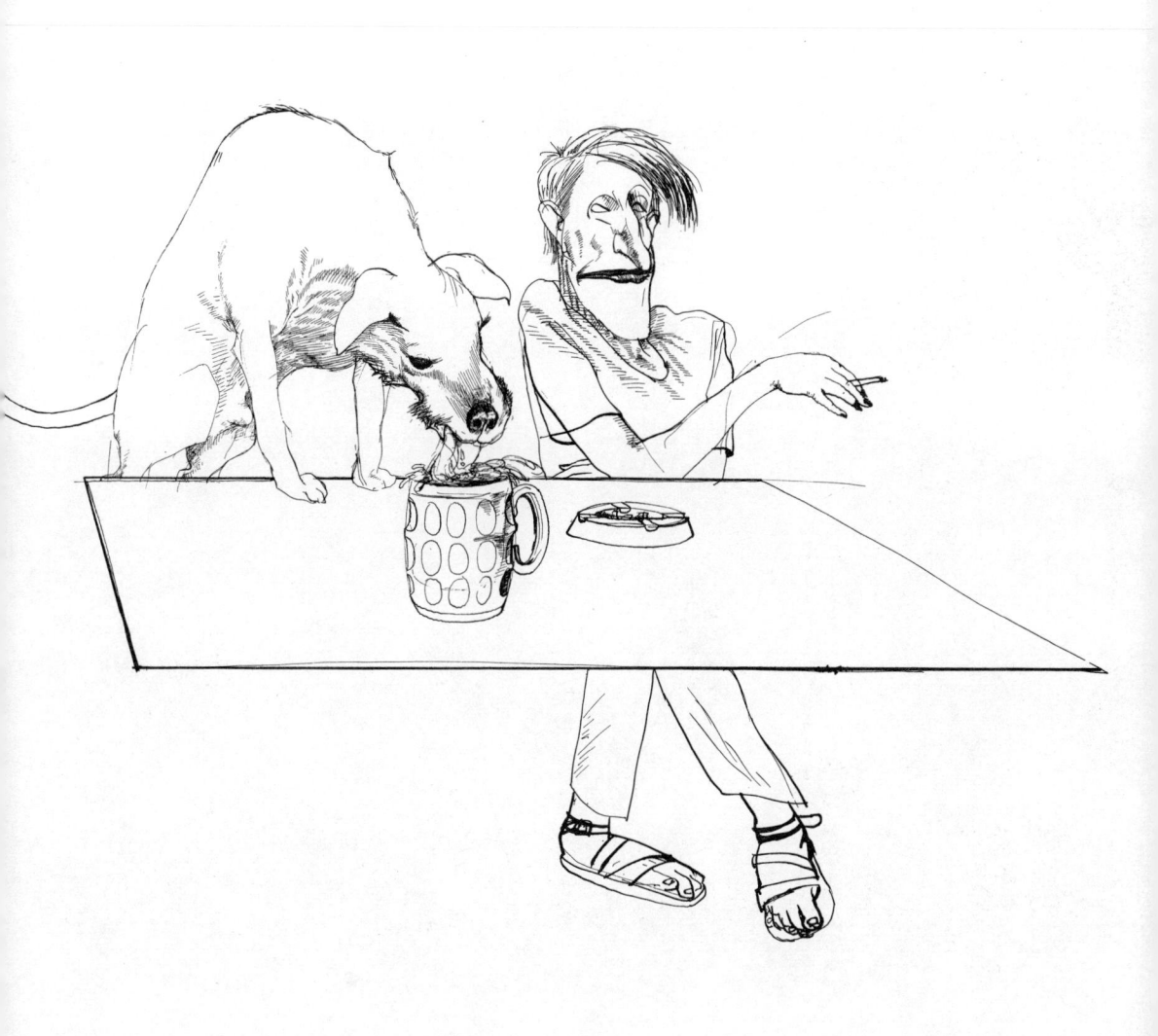

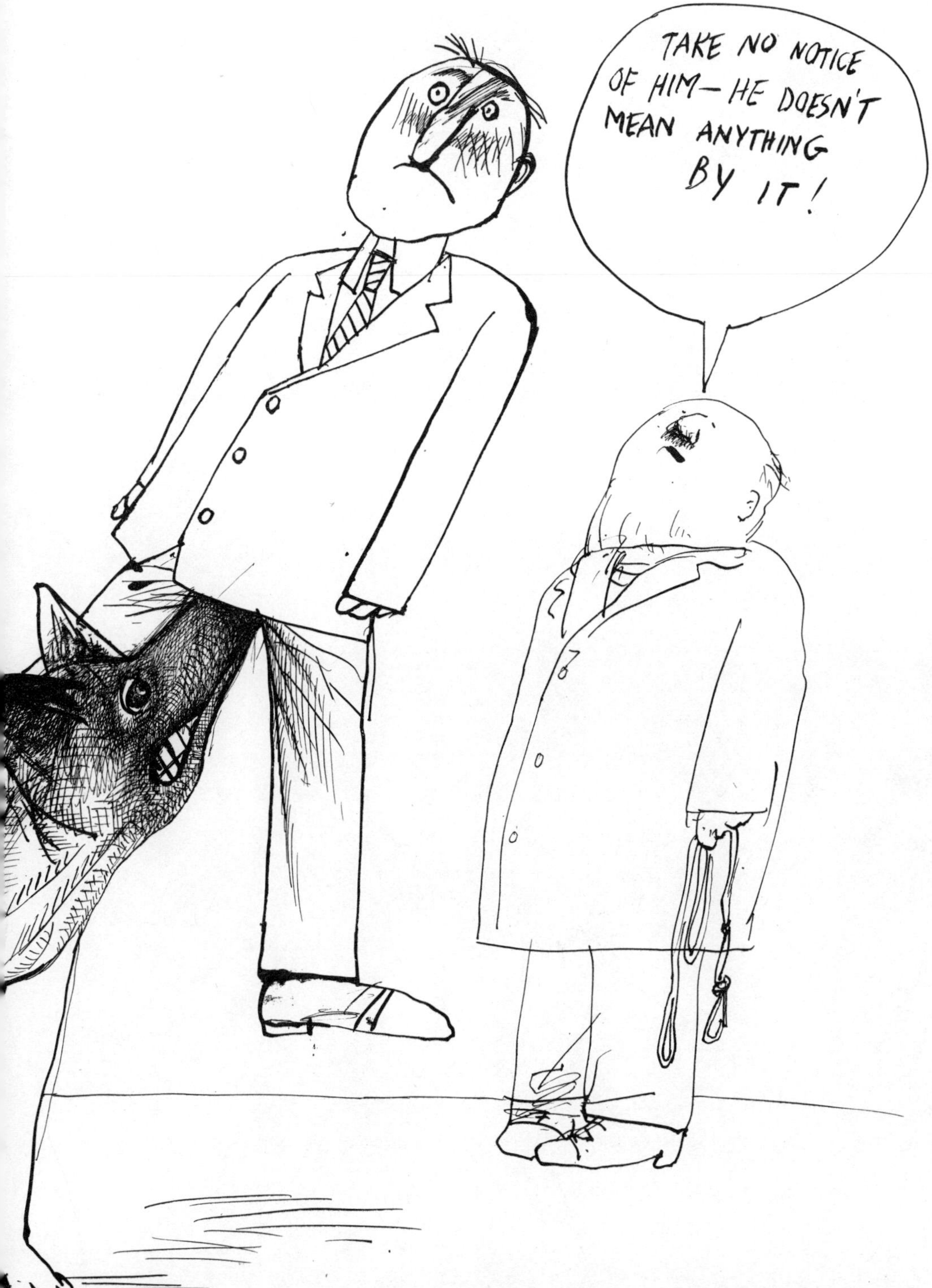
TAKE NO NOTICE OF HIM— HE DOESN'T MEAN ANYTHING BY IT!

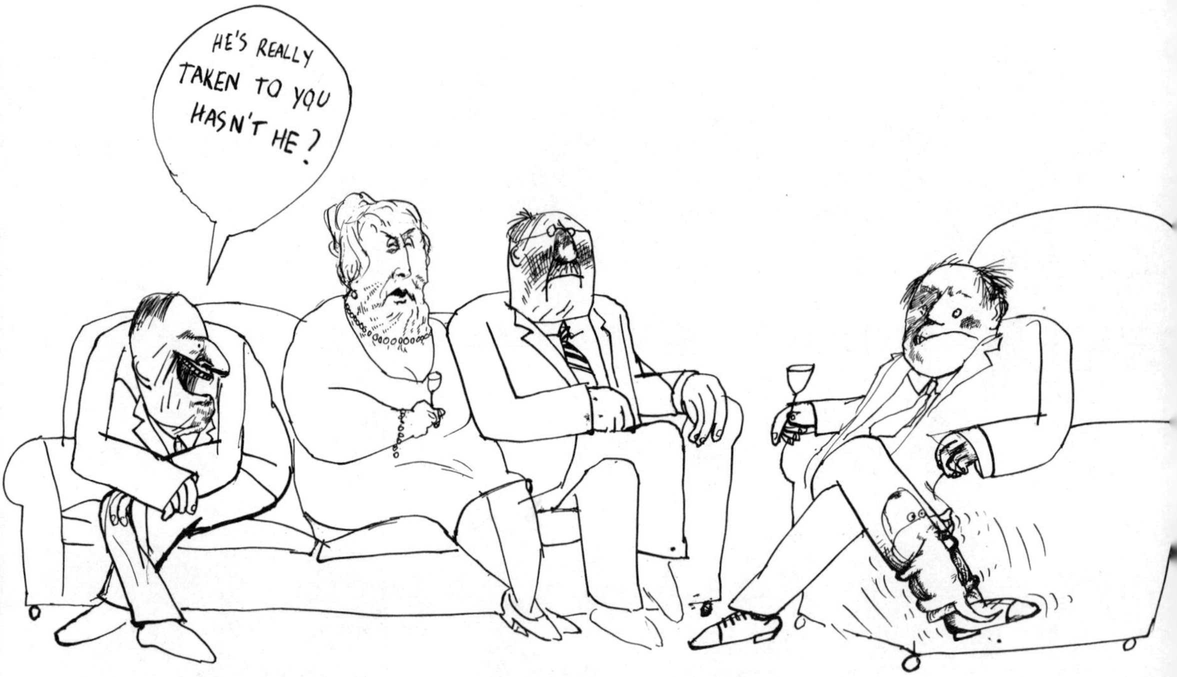
HE'S REALLY TAKEN TO YOU HASN'T HE?

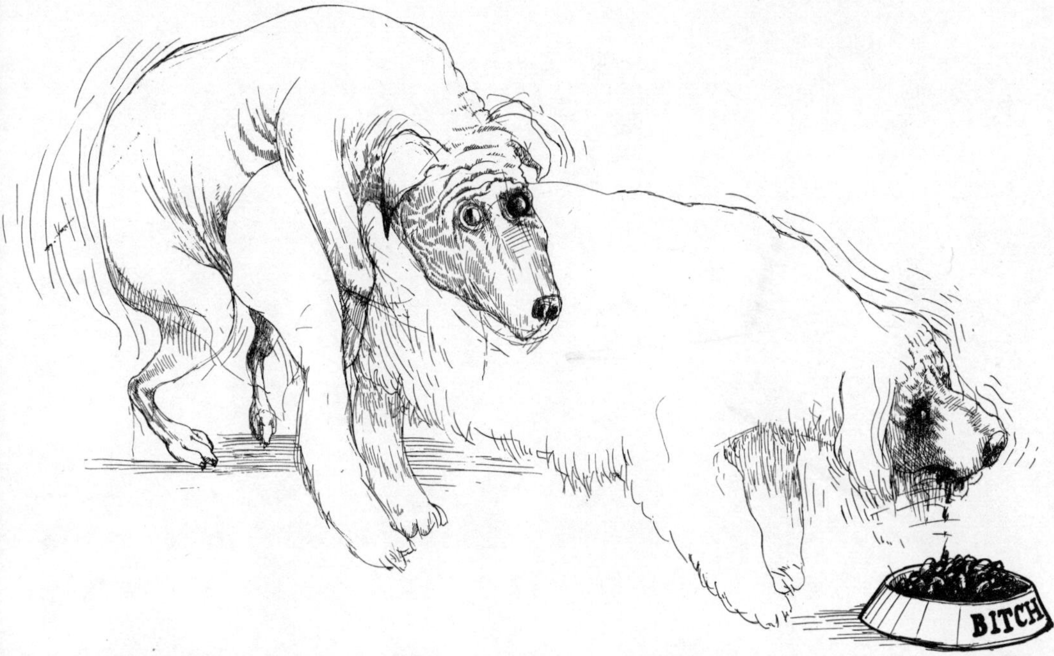
BITCH